The Sainsbury Book of

PRESSURE COOKING
Sue Probert

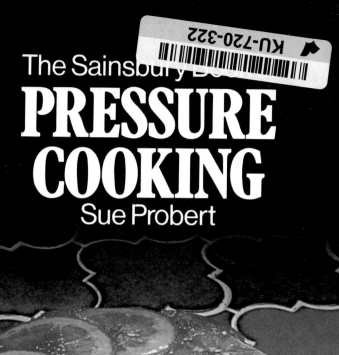

CONTENTS

Published exclusively for
J. Sainsbury Limited
Stamford Street, London SE1 9LL
by Cathay Books
59 Grosvenor Street, London W1

First published 1980

© Cathay Books 1980
ISBN 0 86178 049 3

Printed in Hong Kong

INTRODUCTION

A pressure cooker is one of the most useful items in the modern kitchen. It can be used to produce a variety of tasty dishes – including soups, casseroles, puddings and preserves – in a fraction of the usual time.

Under normal conditions, most liquids reach a maximum temperature of 100°C (212°F) when they boil and give off steam. A pressure cooker is designed to harness this steam, which leads to a rise in pressure and a corresponding increase in temperature. Pressure weights enable the pressure to be controlled. At High (15 lb) pressure a temperature of 122°C (252°F) is reached inside the cooker. The combined effect of the raised temperature and the increased pressure, forcing the steam through the food, reduces the cooking time.

Most pressure cookers have three pressure settings. High (15 lb) pressure is suitable for most cooking purposes; Medium (10 lb) pressure is best for softening fruit for jams; Low (5 lb) pressure is most suitable for cooking steamed puddings.

As pressure cookers vary in design it is essential to follow the manufacturer's instructions for using your cooker, especially with regard to methods of bringing to pressure and reducing pressure after cooking.

For the recipes in this book timing must begin as soon as the required pressure is reached. This is indicated by a 'hissing' noise or movement of the pressure weight. Pressure cooking times are short and therefore often crucial, so always time carefully.

NOTES

Standard spoon measurements are used in all recipes
1 tablespoon = one 15 ml spoon
1 teaspoon   = one 5 ml spoon
All spoon measures are level.

Fresh herbs are used unless otherwise stated. If unobtainable substitute a bouquet garni of the equivalent dried herbs, or use dried herbs instead but halve the quantities stated.

Use freshly ground black pepper where pepper is specified.

For all recipes, quantities are given in both metric and imperial measures. Follow either set but not a mixture of both, because they are not interchangeable.

Chicken Broth

1 chicken carcass
1 potato
1 onion
1 carrot
1 celery stick, sliced
pinch of mixed dried
   herbs
600 ml (1 pint)
   water
salt and pepper
600 ml (1 pint) milk
1 tablespoon chopped
   parsley

Take all the meat off the carcass and set aside.

Put the vegetables in a perforated basket and place in the pressure cooker. Put the carcass in the cooker. Add the herbs, water, and salt and pepper to taste.

Seal the cooker and heat to high pressure. Cook for 20 minutes. Reduce the pressure quickly.

Lift out the basket and chop or mash the vegetables. Strain the liquid and return to the cooker. Add the vegetables, chicken meat, milk and parsley and bring to the boil.

Pour into individual warmed soup bowls and serve hot, with crusty bread.
Serves 4

Dutch Pea Soup

175 g (6 oz) dried
  split peas
25 g (1 oz) butter
1 onion, chopped
1 celery stick,
  chopped
1.2 litres (2 pints)
  chicken stock
1 pork knuckle
1 teaspoon sugar
salt and pepper
1 tablespoon chopped
  mint
2 frankfurters, thinly
  sliced
chopped mint to
  garnish

Cover the peas with boiling water
and leave to stand for 45 minutes;
drain.

Melt the butter in the pressure
cooker, add the onion and fry gently
until transparent. Add the celery,
stock, pork knuckle, sugar, and salt
and pepper to taste.

Seal the cooker and heat to high
pressure. Cook for 20 minutes.
Reduce the pressure quickly.

Remove the pork knuckle, cut off
any meat, chop finely and set aside.

Sieve the soup or work in an
electric blender until smooth. Return
to the cooker, add the pork, mint
and frankfurters and reheat gently.
Check the seasoning. Pour into a
warmed soup tureen and sprinkle
with chopped mint to serve.
Serves 4 to 6

Corn and Bacon Chowder

25 g (1 oz) butter
1 large onion,
    chopped
125 g (4 oz) bacon,
    derinded and
    chopped
1 large potato, diced
1 x 227 g (8 oz)
    packet frozen
    sweetcorn
600 ml (1 pint)
    chicken stock
salt and pepper
600 ml (1 pint) milk
2 tablespoons
    chopped parsley
75 g (3 oz) Cheddar
    cheese, grated
    (optional)
chopped parsley to
    garnish

Melt the butter in the pressure
cooker, add the onion and bacon and
fry gently for 4 to 5 minutes. Add
the potato, sweetcorn, stock, and salt
and pepper to taste.

Seal the cooker and heat to high
pressure. Cook for 4 minutes.
Reduce the pressure at room
temperature.

Add the milk, parsley and cheese,
if using, and reheat gently; do not
boil. Check the seasoning. Pour into
a warmed soup tureen and sprinkle
with chopped parsley to serve.

Serves 4 to 6

Sherried Oxtail Soup

1 tablespoon oil
1 oxtail, cut into
    pieces
1 onion, chopped
2 carrots, sliced
2 celery sticks, sliced
½ teaspoon dried
    mixed herbs
2 tablespoons tomato
    purée
salt and pepper
1.2 litres (2 pints)
    beef stock
1 tablespoon
    cornflour
4 tablespoons sherry
1 tablespoon lemon
    juice
4-6 tablespoons
    cream to serve

Heat the oil in the pressure cooker, add the oxtail and fry, turning, until evenly browned. Pour off any excess fat. Add the onion to the cooker and continue frying for 2 to 3 minutes. Add the carrots, celery, herbs, tomato purée, and salt and pepper to taste. Pour in all but 2 tablespoons of the stock.

Seal the cooker and heat to high pressure. Cook for 45 minutes. Reduce the pressure at room temperature.

Take out the oxtail and cut the meat from the bones; chop finely. Skim any excess fat from the soup. Mash the vegetables in the cooker and add the meat.

Blend the cornflour with the remaining stock, stir into the soup and bring to the boil. Cook, stirring, until thickened. Add the sherry and lemon juice. Pour into individual warmed soup bowls. Top each serving with a swirl of cream.
Serves 4 to 6

Lentil Soup

175 g (6 oz) dried
  lentils
1.2 litres (2 pints)
  water
1 small pork knuckle
1 onion, chopped
1 carrot, sliced
1 clove garlic, crushed
1 teaspoon tomato
  purée
1 celery stick, sliced
salt and pepper
chopped parsley to
  garnish

Place all the ingredients in the pressure cooker, adding salt and pepper to taste. Seal the cooker and heat to high pressure. Cook for 15 minutes. Reduce the pressure quickly.

Remove the pork knuckle, cut off any meat and chop finely; set aside.

Sieve the soup or work in an electric blender until smooth. Return to the cooker, add the meat and reheat gently. Pour into a warmed soup tureen and sprinkle with chopped parsley to serve.
Serves 4 to 6

Leek, Lamb and Potato Soup

500 g (1 lb) middle
  or best end of neck
  lamb chops
500 g (1 lb) leeks,
  thickly sliced
500 g (1 lb) potatoes,
  thickly sliced
600 ml (1 pint) water
salt and pepper
600 ml (1 pint) milk
2 tablespoons
  chopped parsley

Place the meat in the pressure cooker. Add the leeks, potatoes, water, and salt and pepper to taste.

Seal the cooker and heat to high pressure. Cook for 20 minutes. Reduce the pressure quickly.

Remove any loose bones. Add the milk and parsley and check the seasoning. Reheat gently and pour into a warmed soup tureen to serve.
Serves 4 to 6

Celery and Cheese Soup

25 g (1 oz) butter
1 onion, chopped
1 head of celery,
    thinly sliced
600 ml (1 pint) stock
    or water
¼ teaspoon dried
    thyme
salt and pepper
2 teaspoons cornflour
600 ml (1 pint) milk
125 g (4 oz) Cheddar
    cheese, grated
3-4 tablespoons
    natural low-fat
    yogurt
celery leaves to
    garnish

Melt the butter in the pressure cooker, add the onion and celery and fry gently until transparent. Add the stock or water, thyme, and salt and pepper to taste.

Seal the cooker and heat to high pressure. Cook for 10 minutes. Reduce the pressure quickly.

Blend the cornflour with a little of the milk. Add the remaining milk to the soup and bring to the boil. Stir in the cornflour and bring back to the boil. Cook, stirring, until thickened.

Stir in the cheese and yogurt and reheat gently; do not boil. Pour into a warmed soup tureen and garnish with celery leaves to serve.
Serves 4 to 6

Carrot and Orange Soup

25 g (1 oz) butter
1 onion, chopped
1 clove garlic, crushed
1 potato, chopped
750 g (1½ lb)
  carrots, sliced
1 teaspoon tomato
  purée
grated rind and juice
  of 2 oranges
2 tablespoons orange
  squash
1.2 litres (2 pints)
  chicken stock
salt and pepper
4-6 tablespoons
  cream to serve

Melt the butter in the pressure cooker, add the onion and garlic and fry gently until transparent. Add the remaining ingredients, except the orange rind. Season with salt and pepper to taste.

Seal the cooker and heat to high pressure. Cook for 5 minutes. Reduce the pressure quickly.

Sieve the soup or work in an electric blender until smooth. Return to the cooker, add the orange rind and reheat gently. Pour into individual warmed soup bowls. Top each serving with a swirl of cream.
Serves 4 to 6

Fish Soup

carrot, sliced
celery stick
teaspoon mixed dried herbs
tablespoons lemon juice
00 ml (1 pint) water
alt and pepper
ish trimmings – bones, skin, etc. (optional)
75 g (6 oz) cod or coley fillet
onion, chopped
50 ml (¼ pint) dry white wine
tomatoes, skinned and chopped
tablespoons chopped parsley or chervil

Place the carrot, celery, herbs, lemon juice and water in the pressure cooker. Add salt and pepper to taste and the fish trimmings, if using.

Seal the cooker and heat to high pressure. Cook for 10 minutes. Reduce the pressure quickly.

Strain the liquid and return to the cooker. Add the fish, onion and wine.

Seal the cooker and heat to high pressure. Cook for 4 minutes. Reduce the pressure quickly.

Flake the fish in the cooker with a fork. Add the tomatoes and parsley or chervil and bring to the boil. Check the seasoning. Pour into a warmed soup tureen to serve.

Serves 4 to 6

Farmhouse Pâté

4 rashers streaky
  bacon, derinded
350 g (12 oz) belly
  of pork, minced
250 g (8 oz) chicken
  livers, minced or
  chopped
1 onion, chopped
1 clove garlic, crushed
1 egg, beaten
1 teaspoon mixed
  dried herbs
4 tablespoons fresh
  breadcrumbs
salt and pepper

Stretch the bacon with the back of a
knife and use to line a 500 g (1 lb)
loaf tin.

Mix the remaining ingredients
together seasoning liberally with salt
and pepper. Turn the mixture into
the prepared tin and cover tightly
with foil.

Place on the trivet in the pressure
cooker and pour in 600 ml (1 pint)
water.

Seal the cooker and heat to high
pressure. Cook for 30 minutes.
Reduce the pressure at room
temperature.

Place a weight on top of the pâté
and leave until cold. Turn out and
serve with crusty French bread.
Serves 4 to 6

Sweet and Sour Spare Ribs

1.5 kg (3 lb) pork
  spare ribs
1 x 397 g (14 oz)
  can tomatoes
1 x 227 g (8 oz) can
  pineapple pieces
1 tablespoon
  Worcestershire
  sauce
3 tablespoons vinegar
1 tablespoon honey
2 tablespoons brown
  sugar
1 teaspoon ground
  cinnamon

Cut through the spare ribs between the bones. Place the tomatoes and pineapple with juice, Worcestershire sauce, vinegar and honey in the pressure cooker and stir well. Add the spare ribs and leave to marinate for 1 to 2 hours.

Seal the cooker and heat to high pressure. Cook for 15 minutes. Reduce the pressure at room temperature.

Transfer the spare ribs to a grill pan. Keep the sauce warm.

Mix together the brown sugar and cinnamon and sprinkle over the ribs. Place under a preheated hot grill until golden brown. Serve hot with the sauce.

Serves 4 to 6

Tuna and Butter Bean Salad

250 g (8 oz) butter
  beans
600 ml (1 pint)
  water
salt and pepper
1 x 198 g (7 oz) can
  tuna fish
2 tablespoons olive
  oil
3 tablespoons wine
  vinegar
pinch of mustard
pinch of sugar
1 onion, chopped
12-14 black olives,
  stoned and halved
1 tablespoon chopped
  parsley
lettuce leaves to serve

Place the butter beans in a bowl,
cover with boiling water and leave to
stand for 30 minutes. Drain and place
in the pressure cooker. Add the
water and a pinch of salt.

Seal the cooker and heat to high
pressure. Cook for 20 minutes.
Reduce the pressure at room
temperature.

Drain the oil from the tuna into a
large bowl. Add the olive oil,
vinegar, mustard, sugar, and salt and
pepper to taste. Beat thoroughly.

Drain the beans and add to the
dressing while still warm. Toss
thoroughly, then add the tuna,
onion, olives and parsley; mix well.

Just before serving, arrange the
lettuce on a serving plate. Toss the
salad again and pile onto the lettuce.
Serves 4

Seafood Pasta

175 g (6 oz) smoked
  haddock
175 g (6 oz) cod
  fillet
1 onion, quartered
salt and pepper
250 g (8 oz)
  macaroni
1.2 litres (2 pints)
  boiling water
1 tablespoon oil
3 tablespoons sherry
1 x 298 g (10½ oz)
  can condensed
  cream of
  mushroom soup
2 tablespoons
  chopped parsley
parsley sprigs to
  garnish

Butter the unperforated basket of the
pressure cooker. Place the fish and
onion in the basket and season well
with salt and pepper. Stand the
basket in the cooker.

Put the macaroni, 1 teaspoon salt,
the boiling water and oil into the
cooker and stir well. Seal the cooker
and heat to high pressure. Cook for
5 minutes. Reduce the pressure at
room temperature.

Lift out the unperforated basket.
Drain and rinse the macaroni, return
to the cooker and add the sherry and
soup. Mix well and bring to the boil.

Flake the fish and break up the
onion. Add to the cooker with the
chopped parsley; stir well. Check the
seasoning and transfer to a warmed
serving dish. Serve immediately,
garnished with parsley sprigs.
Serves 4

Rillettes

150 ml (¼ pint)
    cider
1 clove garlic, halved
1 teaspoon sage
½ teaspoon rosemary
pinch of grated
    nutmeg
350 g (12 oz) belly
    pork, sliced
1 pork knuckle
salt and pepper
parsley sprigs to
    garnish

Put the cider, garlic, sage, rosemary and nutmeg into the pressure cooker. Put the trivet in the cooker, lay the pork and knuckle on top and season well with salt and pepper.

Seal the cooker and heat to high pressure. Cook for 30 minutes. Reduce the pressure quickly.

Remove any rind and bone from the pork and cut the meat from the knuckle. Break the meat into pieces and divide between 4 individual serving dishes. Strain the cooking liquor over the meat. Leave in the refrigerator until set.

Garnish with parsley sprigs and serve with toast.

Serves 4

Braised Kidneys with Dubonnet

25 g (1 oz) butter
350 g (12 oz) ox
   kidney, thinly
   sliced
2 rashers bacon,
   derinded and
   chopped
1 onion, chopped
6 tablespoons water
3 tablespoons
   Dubonnet
2 tablespoons tomato
   ketchup
salt and pepper
1 teaspoon cornflour
500 g (1 lb)
   potatoes, boiled
   and mashed
chopped parsley to
   garnish

Melt the butter in the pressure cooker, add the kidney, bacon and onion and fry for 2 minutes. Stir in 4 tablespoons of the water, the Dubonnet, ketchup, and salt and pepper to taste.

Seal the cooker and heat to high pressure. Cook for 7 minutes. Reduce the pressure quickly. Blend the cornflour with the remaining water, stir into the sauce and cook, stirring, until thickened.

Place the potato in a piping bag fitted with a large fluted nozzle and pipe a border around the edges of 4 individual ovenproof serving dishes. Place under a preheated hot grill until browned.

Spoon the kidneys into the centre and sprinkle with parsley to serve.
Serves 4

Stuffed Peppers

4 red or green peppers
250 g (8 oz) minced
  beef
4 tablespoons fresh
  breadcrumbs
1 onion, chopped
2 tablespoons tomato
  ketchup
1 teaspoon
  Worcestershire
  sauce
50 g (2 oz) Cheddar
  cheese, grated
salt and pepper
150 ml (¼ pint) beef
  stock or water

Cut the stalk end off the peppers and scoop out the seeds; reserve the 'lids'.

Mix together the beef, bread-crumbs, onion, ketchup, Worcester-shire sauce, cheese and salt and pepper to taste. Fill the peppers with this mixture, pressing down well.

Stand the peppers and the 'lids' on the trivet in the pressure cooker. Pour in the stock or water.

Seal the cooker and heat to high pressure. Cook for 15 minutes. Reduce the pressure at room temperature.

Transfer the peppers to a warmed serving dish and spoon over the liquor. Put the 'lids' on the peppers to serve.

Serves 4

MAIN-COURSE DISHES

Irish Stew

1 kg (2 lb) middle
  neck of lamb
1 kg (2 lb) potatoes,
  halved
4 onions, quartered
4 carrots, quartered
300 ml (½ pint)
  water
salt and pepper
chopped parsley to
  garnish

Place the meat in the pressure cooker. Arrange the vegetables on top, pour in the water, and add salt and pepper to taste.

Seal the cooker and heat to high pressure. Cook for 20 minutes. Reduce the pressure at room temperature.

Check the seasoning and transfer to a warmed serving dish. Sprinkle with parsley to serve.

Serves 4

Lamb Goulash

1 tablespoon oil
1 kg (2 lb) best end
 of neck lamb chops
2 onions, sliced
1 clove garlic, crushed
2 tablespoons paprika
500 g (1lb) tomatoes,
 skinned and
 chopped, or
 1 x 397 g (14 oz)
 can tomatoes
1 teaspoon dried
 mixed herbs
½ teaspoon caraway
 seeds (optional)
salt and pepper
150 ml (¼ pint)
 stock or water
1 tablespoon cornflour
142 ml (5 fl oz)
 fresh sour cream

Heat the oil in the pressure cooker, add the chops and fry on both sides until browned. Add the onions and garlic and cook until transparent, then add the paprika and mix well.

Stir in the tomatoes with their juice, herbs, caraway seeds, if using, and salt and pepper to taste. Pour in all but 2 tablespoons of the stock or water.

Seal the cooker and heat to high pressure. Cook for 15 minutes. Reduce the pressure quickly.

Blend the cornflour with the remaining water, stir into the sauce and bring to the boil. Cook, stirring, until thickened. Add the sour cream and reheat gently; do not boil. Check the seasoning.

Transfer to a warmed serving dish and serve with buttered noodles or boiled rice.
Serves 4

Pork and Cabbage Casserole

25 g (1 oz) butter
4 spare rib pork
  chops
150 ml (¼ pint)
  water
1 teaspoon made
  mustard
2 tablespoons vinegar
1 teaspoon caraway
  seeds
salt and pepper
1 onion, sliced
500 g (1 lb) cabbage,
  thickly sliced
750 g (1½ lb)
  potatoes, thickly
  sliced
chopped parsley to
  garnish

Melt the butter in the pressure
cooker, add the chops and fry until
browned on both sides. Add the
water, mustard, vinegar, caraway
seeds, and salt and pepper to taste.

Seal the cooker and heat to high
pressure. Cook for 12 minutes.
Reduce the pressure quickly.

Arrange the onion, cabbage and
potatoes in layers on the pork,
seasoning each layer liberally with
salt and pepper.

Seal the cooker and heat to high
pressure. Cook for 3 minutes.
Reduce the pressure quickly.

Transfer to a warmed serving dish
and sprinkle with parsley to serve.
Serves 4

Spiced Pork Chops

1 tablespoon oil
4 pork chops
1 tablespoon honey
1 tablespoon sweet
  chutney
2 tablespoons vinegar
1 clove garlic, crushed
1 teaspoon ground
  mixed spice
150 ml (¼ pint)
  water
1 x 298 g (10½ oz)
  can condensed
  tomato soup
salt and pepper
watercress sprigs to
  garnish

Heat the oil in the pressure cooker,
add the chops and fry until browned
on both sides; remove from the
cooker and keep warm. Stir in the
remaining ingredients, with salt and
pepper to taste, and return the chops
to the cooker.

Seal the cooker and heat to high
pressure. Cook for 15 minutes.
Reduce the pressure at room
temperature.

Transfer to a warmed serving dish,
garnish with watercress and serve
with boiled rice.
Serves 4

Braised Pork with Sage

25 g (1 oz) butter
4 spare rib pork
  chops
500 g (1 lb) onions,
  sliced
1 tablespoon dried
  sage
300 ml (½ pint)
  orange juice
salt and pepper
1 tablespoon cornflour,
  blended with
  2 tablespoons
  water
1 orange, sliced, to
  garnish

Melt the butter in the pressure
cooker, add the chops and fry until
well browned on both sides. Add the
onions and continue frying for 4 to
5 minutes. Add the sage, orange
juice, and salt and pepper to taste.

Seal the cooker and heat to high
pressure. Cook for 12 minutes.
Reduce the pressure at room
temperature.

Stir the blended cornflour into the
sauce and bring to the boil. Cook,
stirring, until thickened.

Transfer to a warmed serving dish
and garnish with orange slices.
Serves 4

23

French Braised Brisket

1 tablespoon oil
1 kg (2 lb) piece of
   beef brisket
2 onions, quartered
1 clove garlic, crushed
2 celery sticks,
   thickly sliced
4 carrots, halved
1 small swede, diced
1 leek, sliced
150 ml (¼ pint) red
   wine
150 ml (¼ pint)
   water
2 tablespoons tomato
   purée
1 teaspoon dried
   mixed herbs
salt and pepper
1 tablespoon cornflour

Heat the oil in the pressure cooker, add the meat and brown on all sides. Remove the meat.

Put the onions and garlic in the cooker and fry gently for 1 to 2 minutes. Add all the vegetables and place the meat on top.

Combine the wine, half the water, tomato purée, herbs, and salt and pepper to taste. Pour over the meat.

Seal the cooker and heat to high pressure. Cook for 30 minutes. Reduce the pressure at room temperature.

Transfer the meat and vegetables to a warmed serving dish.

Blend the cornflour with the remaining water, stir into the sauce in the cooker and bring to the boil. Cook, stirring, until thickened. Serve with the meat.
Serves 4 to 6

Beef Stew with Dumplings

1 tablespoon oil
750 g (1½ lb)
   stewing steak,
   cubed
2 onions, quartered
2 celery sticks,
   thickly sliced
4 carrots, sliced
2 turnips, diced
300 ml (½ pint) beef
   stock
1 tablespoon tomato
   purée
salt and pepper
DUMPLINGS:
125 g (4 oz)
   self-raising flour
50 g (2 oz) shredded
   suet
3-4 tablespoons
   water

TO GARNISH:
chopped parsley

Heat the oil in the pressure cooker, add the meat and fry until browned all over. Add the remaining ingredients, with salt and pepper to taste, and stir well.

Seal the cooker and heat to high pressure. Cook for 12 minutes. Reduce the pressure quickly.

To make the dumplings: Sift the flour and a pinch of salt into a bowl. Stir in the suet and enough water to make a soft dough. Knead lightly, then form into small balls. Place on top of the stew.

Seal the cooker but do not fit the weight. Steam for 10 minutes.

Transfer to a warmed serving dish and sprinkle with parsley to serve.
Serves 4

Steak and Kidney Pudding

FILLING:

2 tablespoons plain
    flour
salt and pepper
500 g (1 lb)
    stewing steak,
    cubed
125 g (4 oz) ox
    kidney, sliced
1 tablespoon oil
1 onion, chopped
1 tablespoon tomato
    purée
150 ml (¼ pint) beef
    stock

PASTRY:

250 g (8 oz)
    self-raising flour
125 g (4 oz)
    shredded suet
pinch of mixed dried
    herbs
6-7 tablespoons water

Season the flour with salt and pepper and use to coat the steak and kidney.

Heat the oil in the pressure cooker, add the steak and kidney and fry until evenly browned. Stir in the onion, tomato purée and stock. Seal the cooker and heat to high pressure. Cook for 15 minutes. Reduce the pressure quickly.

Strain all but 4 tablespoons of the liquor from the meat and reserve. Leave to cool.

Sift together the flour and a pinch of salt. Stir in the suet, herbs and enough water to make a soft dough. Knead lightly.

Set aside one quarter of the pastry. Roll out the remainder and use to line a greased 1 litre (1½ pint) pudding basin. Fill with the meat mixture.

Roll out the reserved pastry to make a lid, dampen the edge and put in position. Press the edges together to seal.

Cover with two sheets of greaseproof paper or a sheet of foil, making a pleat across the centre. Secure with string.

Stand the basin on the trivet in the cleaned pressure cooker, containing 1.75 litres (3 pints) boiling water. Seal the cooker but do not fit the weight. Steam for 20 minutes.

Put the pressure weight on and heat to low pressure. Cook for 30 minutes. Reduce the pressure at room temperature.

Turn out the pudding onto a warmed serving dish. Reheat the reserved liquor and serve separately.
Serves 4

Meat Balls in Tomato Sauce

750 g (1½ lb)
  minced beef
1 onion, finely
  chopped
50 g (2 oz)
  long-grain rice
¼ teaspoon chilli
  powder (optional)
salt and pepper
1 egg, beaten
1 tablespoon oil
150 ml (¼ pint)
  water
1 x 298 g (10½ oz)
  can condensed
  tomato soup
parsley sprigs to
  garnish

Mix together the beef, onion, rice and chilli powder, if using, and salt and pepper to taste. Bind the mixture with the egg, then divide into 8 or 12 pieces and form into balls.

Heat the oil in the pressure cooker, add the meat balls and fry until evenly browned. Mix together the water and soup and pour over the meat balls.

Seal the cooker and heat to high pressure. Cook for 15 minutes. Reduce the pressure at room temperature.

Transfer to a warmed serving dish and garnish with parsley. Serve with pasta.
Serves 4

Stuffed Marrow

1 tablespoon oil
350 g (12 oz)
    minced beef
1 onion, chopped
1 tablespoon tomato
    purée
1 teaspoon
    Worcestershire
    sauce
50 g (2 oz) dried
    lentils
300 ml (½ pint) beef
    stock
salt and pepper
1 short, plump
    marrow, weighing
    about 750 g
    (1½ lb), peeled,
    halved and seeded
25 g (1 oz) butter

Heat the oil in the pressure cooker, add the beef and onion and fry until just beginning to brown. Stir in the tomato purée, Worcestershire sauce, lentils, half the stock, and salt and pepper to taste. Bring to the boil, stirring constantly, lower the heat and simmer for 3 to 4 minutes.

Spoon the mixture into one half of the marrow and place the other half on top. Place on the trivet in the cooker and pour in the remaining stock.

Seal the cooker and heat to high pressure. Cook for 11 minutes. Reduce the pressure at room temperature.

Transfer the marrow to a warmed serving dish and spoon over the liquor. Dot with butter to serve.
Serves 4

Potted Beef

500 g (1 lb) stewing
   steak, thinly sliced
300 ml (½ pint)
   water
1 pork knuckle
1 onion, halved
salt and pepper
ground mixed spice
TO GARNISH:
1 tablespoon
   horseradish sauce
4 tablespoons
   whipped cream or
   natural low-fat
   yogurt

Put the meat, water, pork knuckle
and onion in the pressure cooker.
Add salt, pepper and spice to taste.

Seal the cooker and heat to high
pressure. Cook for 30 minutes.
Reduce the pressure at room
temperature.

Remove the knuckle and cut off
any meat. Return the meat to the
cooker, stirring with a fork to break
it up.

Turn the mixture into a tureen or
deep serving dish and leave until
cold. Skim any fat from the surface.

To prepare the garnish: Mix the
horseradish sauce and cream or
yogurt together. Spread over the
beef just before serving.

Serve with a mixed salad and
crusty bread.

Serves 4

Oxtail Casserole

1 tablespoon oil
1 oxtail, cut into
    pieces
2 onions, sliced
2 carrots, sliced
1 swede, diced
2 celery sticks, sliced
½ teaspoon dried
    mixed herbs
450 ml (¾ pint) beef
    stock or water
150 ml (¼ pint) red
    wine
2 tablespoons tomato
    purée
salt and pepper
1 tablespoon lemon
    juice

Heat the oil in the pressure cooker. Add the oxtail and onions and fry until browned. Pour off the excess fat. Add the vegetables, herbs, stock or water, wine, and tomato purée. Season with salt and pepper to taste.

Seal the cooker and heat to high pressure. Cook for 45 minutes. Reduce the pressure at room temperature.

Check the seasoning and add the lemon juice. Transfer to a warmed serving dish.

Serves 4

NOTE: This casserole is best made in advance and allowed to cool so that the fat can be skimmed off. Reheat before serving.

Kidney and Sausage Sauté

1 tablespoon oil
350 g (12 oz) ox
    kidney, sliced
50 g (2 oz) bacon,
    derinded and
    chopped
2 onions, sliced
2 celery sticks, sliced
125 g (4 oz) button
    mushrooms
125 g (4 oz) pork
    sausages
1 x 397 g (14 oz)
    can tomatoes
1 tablespoon
    redcurrant jelly
salt and pepper
1 tablespoon
    cornflour, blended
    with 2 tablespoons
    water
chopped parsley to
    garnish

Heat the oil in the pressure cooker, add the kidney, bacon and onions and fry for 5 to 7 minutes or until browned. Add the celery, mushrooms, sausages, tomatoes with their juice and redcurrant jelly. Season with salt and pepper to taste.

Seal the cooker and heat to high pressure. Cook for 5 minutes. Reduce the pressure at room temperature.

Remove the sausages, cut each into 3 pieces and return to the cooker.

Stir in the blended cornflour and bring to the boil. Cook, stirring, until thickened. Check the seasoning and transfer to a warmed serving dish.

Serve with buttered noodles or boiled rice.

Serves 4

Liver and Bacon Casserole

1 tablespoon oil
500 g (1 lb) lambs'
   liver, sliced
1 tablespoon plain
   flour
125 g (4 oz) streaky
   bacon, derinded
   and chopped
2 onions, chopped
300 ml (1/2 pint) beef
   stock
2 tablespoons tomato
   ketchup
salt and pepper
chopped parsley to
   garnish

Heat the oil in the pressure cooker. Coat the liver with the flour, add to the cooker and fry for 2 to 3 minutes on each side; remove and set aside.

Add the bacon and onions to the cooker and fry gently until soft. Add the stock, tomato ketchup, and salt and pepper to taste. Return the liver to the cooker.

Seal the cooker and heat to high pressure. Cook for 4 minutes. Reduce the pressure at room temperature.

Check the seasoning. Transfer to a warmed serving dish and sprinkle with parsley.
Serves 4

31

Braised Stuffed Hearts

4 lambs' hearts
125 g (4 oz) bacon,
 derinded and
 chopped
1 x 99 g (3½ oz)
 packet thyme and
 parsley stuffing
 mix
1 egg, beaten
3-5 tablespoons
 water
salt and pepper
600 ml (1 pint) stock
1 onion, sliced
1 tablespoon
 cornflour

Rinse the hearts thoroughly and cut out the central tubes and membranes.

Place the bacon in a small pan over moderate heat and fry in its own fat until lightly browned.

Put the stuffing and bacon in a bowl, add the egg and enough water to make a soft mixture. Season with salt and pepper to taste. Use to stuff the hearts, pressing down well.

Place the hearts in the pressure cooker and pour in all but 2 tablespoons of the stock. Add the onion. Seal the cooker and heat to high pressure. Cook for 30 minutes. Reduce the pressure quickly.

Transfer the hearts to a warmed serving dish and keep hot.

Blend the cornflour with the remaining stock, stir into the sauce and bring to the boil. Cook, stirring, until thickened. Spoon some of the sauce over the hearts and serve the rest separately. Serve with French beans or peas.
Serves 4

Tripe and Onions

500 g (1 lb) tripe,
cut into 2.5 cm
(1 inch) strips
500 g (1 lb) onions,
sliced
125 g (4 oz) bacon,
derinded and
chopped
300 ml (½ pint)
cider or water
bouquet garni
salt and pepper
1 tablespoon
cornflour, blended
with 150 ml
(¼ pint) milk
parsley sprigs to
garnish

Place the tripe, onions, bacon, cider
or water, bouquet garni, and salt and
pepper to taste in the pressure
cooker.

Seal the cooker and heat to high
pressure. Cook for 20 minutes.
Reduce the pressure at room
temperature.

Stir in the blended cornflour and
bring to the boil. Cook, stirring,
until thickened. Remove the bouquet
garni and check the seasoning.

Transfer to a warmed serving dish
and garnish with parsley.
Serves 4

Bohemian Chicken

25 g (1 oz) butter
4 chicken quarters
2 rashers bacon,
    derinded and
    chopped
2 onions, quartered
1 x 397 g (14 oz)
    can tomatoes
1 red pepper, cored,
    seeded and sliced
1 teaspoon paprika
salt and pepper
HERB DUMPLINGS:
50 g (2 oz)
    self-raising flour
25 g (1 oz) shredded
    suet
1 teaspoon dried
    mixed herbs
2-3 tablespoons
    water

Melt the butter in the pressure cooker, add the chicken quarters and fry until golden all over. Add the bacon and onions and cook for 3 to 4 minutes. Stir in the tomatoes with their juice, red pepper, paprika, and salt and pepper to taste.

Seal the cooker and heat to high pressure. Cook for 7 minutes. Reduce the pressure quickly.

To make the dumplings: Sift the flour into a bowl and stir in the suet, herbs, and salt and pepper to taste. Add enough water to form a soft dough, knead lightly and form into 8 small balls. Place on top of the chicken in the cooker.

Put the lid on the cooker, but do not fit the weight. Steam over a low heat for 12 to 15 minutes until the dumplings are light and well risen.

Transfer the chicken to a warmed serving dish, pour over the vegetables and juice and surround with the dumplings.
Serves 4

Madras Chicken

1 tablespoon oil
4 chicken quarters
1 onion, chopped
1 clove garlic, crushed
1 cooking apple,
    peeled, cored and
    sliced
1 chilli, chopped
1 tablespoon curry
    powder
1 tablespoon mango
    chutney
150 ml (¼ pint)
    chicken stock
1 banana, thinly
    sliced

Heat the oil in the pressure cooker, add the chicken quarters and fry until golden brown all over. Remove from the cooker and keep warm.

Add the onion, garlic, apple and chilli to the cooker and fry gently for 4 to 5 minutes. Sprinkle in the curry powder and cook for 1 to 2 minutes.

Add the chutney and stock and return the chicken to the cooker. Seal the cooker and heat to high pressure. Cook for 7 minutes. Reduce the pressure at room temperature.

Stir in the banana and transfer to a warmed serving dish. Serve with boiled rice.
Serves 4

Normandy Chicken

25 g (1 oz) butter
1 x 1.5 kg (3-3½ lb)
    oven-ready chicken
300 ml (½ pint)
    cider
2 onions, quartered
2 cooking apples,
    peeled and
    quartered
salt and pepper
2 tablespoons
    cornflour, blended
    with 4 tablespoons
    water
114 ml (4 fl oz)
    double cream

TO GARNISH:
25 g (1 oz) butter
2 dessert apples,
    cored and sliced
2 tablespoons lemon
    juice

Melt the butter in the pressure cooker, add the chicken and brown on all sides. Add the cider, onions, apples, and salt and pepper to taste.

Seal the cooker and heat to high pressure. Cook for 15 minutes. Reduce the pressure at room temperature. Remove the chicken and keep hot.

Purée the cooking liquor in an electric blender or rub through a sieve and return to the cooker. Stir in the blended cornflour and bring to the boil. Cook, stirring, until thickened. Stir in the cream and reheat gently; do not boil. Check the seasoning.

To prepare the garnish: Melt the butter in a frying pan, add the apples and fry for about 1 minute on each side. Sprinkle with the lemon juice.

Slice the chicken and arrange on a warmed serving dish. Spoon over some of the sauce and garnish with the apple slices. Serve the remaining sauce separately.
Serves 4 to 6

Mustard Rabbit in Celery Sauce

4 rabbit quarters
25 g (1 oz) butter
2 onions, sliced
150 ml (¼ pint)
    water
1 x 298 g (10½ oz)
    can condensed
    celery soup
3 teaspoons French
    mustard
½ teaspoon dried
    sage
125 g (4 oz) mush-
    rooms, sliced
TO GARNISH:
4 rashers bacon,
    derinded

Place the rabbit quarters in the pressure cooker and cover with cold water. Bring to the boil, then drain. Rinse and dry the cooker.

Melt the butter in the cooker, add the rabbit and onions and fry until golden. Add the remaining ingredients.

Seal the cooker and heat to high pressure. Cook for 17 minutes. Reduce the pressure quickly.

Fry the bacon in its own fat in a pan over moderate heat until crisp. Transfer the rabbit and sauce to a warmed serving dish and garnish with the bacon.

Serves 4

Pasta Shells with Tomato and Bacon Sauce

250 g (8 oz) pasta
    shells
1.75 litres (3 pints)
    boiling water
1 tablespoon oil
salt and pepper
SAUCE:
1 tablespoon oil
1 onion, chopped
1 clove garlic, crushed
350 g (12 oz) lean
    bacon, chopped
150 ml (¼ pint)
    water
500 g (1 lb)
    tomatoes, skinned
    and quartered
1 tablespoon cornflour
TO SERVE:
chopped parsley
grated Parmesan
    cheese

Place the pasta, water, oil and 1 teaspoon salt in the pressure cooker and bring to the boil. Seal the cooker and heat to high pressure. Cook for 4 minutes. Reduce the pressure at room temperature. Drain the pasta.

To make the sauce: Heat the oil in the cleaned cooker, add the onion, garlic and bacon and fry gently for 5 minutes. Add all but 2 tablespoons water, and salt and pepper to taste.

Seal the cooker and heat to high pressure. Cook for 5 minutes. Reduce the pressure quickly.

Add the tomatoes and bring to the boil. Blend cornflour with remaining water, stir into the sauce and cook, stirring, until thickened. Add the pasta and simmer for 3 to 4 minutes.

Transfer to a warmed serving dish and sprinkle with parsley. Serve Parmesan cheese separately.

Serves 4

Cod Provençal

1 tablespoon olive oil
1 onion, sliced
1 clove garlic, crushed
1 green pepper, cored,
    seeded and sliced
150 ml (¼ pint)
    water
1 tablespoon tomato
    purée
3-4 tomatoes,
    skinned and
    quartered
750 g (1½ lb) cod
    fillet, cut into
    4 pieces
salt and pepper
3-4 stuffed olives,
    sliced, to garnish

Heat the oil in the pressure cooker, add the onion and garlic and fry gently until transparent. Add the green pepper and continue cooking for 1 to 2 minutes. Stir in the water, tomato purée and tomatoes. Arrange the fish on top and season well with salt and pepper.

Seal the cooker and heat to high pressure. Cook for 4 minutes. Reduce the pressure quickly.

Transfer to a warmed serving dish and garnish with sliced olives.
Serves 4

Fish and Potato Pie

750 g (1½ lb)
    potatoes, grated
1 egg
4 tablespoons milk
250 g (8 oz) cod
    fillet, diced
50 g (2 oz) fresh
    breadcrumbs
1 onion, finely
    chopped
1 tomato, chopped
2 tablespoons
    chopped parsley
125 g (4 oz)
    Cheddar cheese,
    grated
salt and pepper
grated nutmeg
25 g (1 oz) butter
parsley sprigs to
    garnish

Cover the potato with cold water and leave to stand for 2 to 3 minutes; drain well.

Beat the egg and milk together in a bowl. Add the fish, breadcrumbs, onion, tomato, parsley, cheese, potato and salt, pepper and nutmeg to taste, mix well.

Place in a 1.2 litre (2 pint) casserole dish, dot with the butter and cover with foil. Stand the dish on the trivet in the pressure cooker and pour in about 1.2 litres (2 pints) boiling water.

Seal the cooker but do not fit the weight. Steam for 20 minutes. Put the pressure weight on and heat to high pressure. Cook for 30 minutes. Reduce the pressure at room temperature.

Remove the foil from the dish and place the pie under a preheated hot grill until the top is crisp and brown. Serve immediately, garnished with parsley.
Serves 4

Soused Mackerel

4 mackerel, cleaned
  and heads removed
1 teaspoon pickling
  spice
600 ml (1 pint)
  water
3 tablespoons vinegar
1 onion, chopped
1 red chilli pepper to
  garnish (optional)

Score the skin of the mackerel and put them in the pressure cooker. Add the remaining ingredients.

Seal the cooker and heat to high pressure. Cook for 4 minutes. Reduce the pressure at room temperature.

Leave the mackerel in the cooking liquor until cold. Transfer to a serving dish and garnish with a chilli pepper if liked. Serve with wholemeal bread.
Serves 4

VEGETABLES & SALADS

Spiced Red Cabbage

1 tablespoon oil
1 onion, sliced
1 cooking apple,
 peeled, cored and
 sliced
2 tablespoons vinegar
4-6 cloves
½ teaspoon caraway
 seeds
1 red cabbage,
 shredded
1 tablespoon
 redcurrant jelly

Heat the oil in the pressure cooker, add the onion and fry for 2 to 3 minutes. Add the remaining ingredients.

Seal the cooker and heat to high pressure. Cook for 4 minutes. Reduce the pressure quickly.

Stir well and transfer to a warmed serving dish.

Serves 4

Neapolitan Celery

1 tablespoon oil
50 g (2 oz)
    spaghetti, broken
    into pieces
1 onion, sliced
1 x 397 g (14 oz)
    can tomatoes
salt and pepper
750 g (1½ lb)
    celery, sliced
175 g (6 oz)
    Cheddar cheese,
    grated
2-3 tablespoons
    chopped mixed
    herbs

Heat the oil in the pressure cooker. Add the spaghetti and toss until evenly coated. Add the onion and tomatoes, with their juice, making sure all the spaghetti is covered. Season with salt and pepper to taste. Layer the celery on top and season well.

Seal the cooker and heat to high pressure. Cook for 6 minutes. Reduce the pressure at room temperature.

Stir in the cheese and herbs and transfer to a warmed serving dish. Serve hot.
Serves 4

Boston Baked Beans

250 g (8 oz) haricot
beans
1 x 397 g (14 oz)
can tomatoes
1 onion, chopped
1 tablespoon black
treacle
1 teaspoon French
mustard
1 tablespoon sugar
125 g (4 oz) salt
pork, chopped
1 tablespoon tomato
purée
300 ml (½ pint)
water
salt and pepper
1 tablespoon
cornflour

Place the haricot beans in a bowl,
cover with boiling water and leave to
soak for 30 minutes; drain.

Put the beans, tomatoes with their
juice, onion, treacle, mustard, sugar,
pork and tomato purée in the
pressure cooker. Add all but
2 tablespoons of the water and
season with salt and pepper to taste.
Stir well.

Seal the cooker and heat to high
pressure. Cook for 20 minutes.
Reduce the pressure at room
temperature.

Blend the cornflour with the
remaining water and stir into the
mixture. Cook, stirring, until
thickened.

Transfer to a warmed serving dish
Serve hot.
Serves 4

Stuffed Cabbage Leaves

8 large cabbage
leaves
25 g (1 oz) butter
1 onion, chopped
350 g (12 oz)
smoked haddock,
skinned and
chopped
75 g (3 oz)
long-grain rice,
cooked
1 tablespoon chopped
parsley
75 g (3 oz) Cheddar
cheese, grated
salt and pepper
150 ml (¼ pint)
water
1 x 298 g (10½ oz)
can condensed
tomato soup

Blanch the cabbage leaves in boiling
water for 2 minutes; drain.

Melt the butter in the pressure
cooker, add the onion and fry for
2 to 3 minutes. Stir in the haddock,
rice, parsley, cheese, and salt and
pepper to taste. Mix well.

Divide the mixture between the
cabbage leaves and roll up, folding in
the sides to make parcels. Place, join
side down, in the cooker. Mix
together the water and soup and
pour into the cooker.

Seal the cooker and heat to high
pressure. Cook for 6 minutes.
Reduce the pressure quickly.

Transfer to a warmed serving dish
Serve hot.
Serves 4

Kidney Beans
in Barbecue Sauce

250 g (8 oz) red
  kidney beans
150 ml (¼ pint)
  stock or water
1 x 298 g (10½ oz)
  can condensed
  tomato soup
½ teaspoon ground
  mixed spice
¼ teaspoon ground
  ginger
1 clove garlic, crushed
½ teaspoon dry
  mustard
2 tablespoons vinegar
2 tablespoons Worces-
  tershire sauce
2 tablespoons sweet
  chutney
1 tablespoon chopped
  rosemary

Cover the kidney beans with boiling
water and leave to soak for
30 minutes. Drain and place in the
pressure cooker. Add the remaining
ingredients and mix well.

Seal the cooker and heat to high
pressure. Cook for 20 minutes.
Reduce the pressure at room
temperature.

Stir well and transfer to a warmed
serving dish. Serve hot.

Serves 4

43

Baked Stuffed Onions

4 large onions
150 ml (¼ pint)
    stock
250 g (8 oz) bacon,
    chopped
½ teaspoon dry
    mustard
1 dessert apple,
    peeled, cored and
    grated
2 tablespoons single
    cream or milk
4 tablespoons fresh
    breadcrumbs
salt and pepper

Place the onions and stock in the pressure cooker. Seal the cooker and heat to high pressure. Cook for 3 minutes. Reduce the pressure quickly.

Lift the onions from the cooker with a slotted spoon, scoop out the insides and chop roughly. Set the onion shells aside.

Place the bacon and chopped onion in a saucepan and heat gently until the bacon fat runs. Increase the heat slightly and fry until the onion is softened. Add the remaining ingredients, with salt and pepper to taste; mix well.

Spoon the stuffing into the onion shells, pressing down well. Return the onions to the cooker.

Seal the cooker and heat to high pressure. Cook for 12 minutes. Reduce the pressure at room temperature.

Transfer the onions to a warmed serving dish and spoon over the cooking liquor. Serve hot.
Serves 4

Braised Marrow and Tomatoes

25 (1 oz) butter
75 g (3 oz) fresh
    breadcrumbs
50 g (2 oz) Cheddar
    cheese, grated
1 teaspoon dried
    thyme
1 tablespoon oil
1 large onion,
    chopped
1 clove garlic, crushed
1 marrow, peeled,
    seeded and diced
350 g (12 oz)
    tomatoes, skinned
    and quartered
4 tablespoons water
salt and pepper
1 tablespoon
    cornflour
tomato slices to
    garnish

Melt the butter in the pressure cooker, add the breadcrumbs and fry until golden brown, stirring constantly. Turn into a bowl, stir in the cheese and thyme and set aside.

Heat the oil in the cleaned pressure cooker, add the onion and garlic and fry gently for 2 to 3 minutes. Add the marrow, tomatoes, 2 tablespoons of the water, and salt and pepper to taste. Stir well.

Seal the cooker and heat to high pressure. Cook for 2 minutes. Reduce the pressure at room temperature.

Blend the cornflour with the remaining water and stir into the sauce. Cook, stirring, until thickened.

Transfer to a shallow ovenproof serving dish and cover with the reserved breadcrumb mixture. Place under a preheated hot grill until golden brown. Serve immediately, garnished with tomato slices.

Serves 4 to 6

Dahl

1 tablespoon oil
1 onion, chopped
1 clove garlic, crushed
¼ teaspoon chilli
   powder
1 teaspoon ground
   cumin
1 teaspoon turmeric
250 g (8 oz) dried
   lentils
600 ml (1 pint)
   water
salt and pepper
3 tablespoons natural
   low-fat yogurt
1 tablespoon mango
   chutney

Heat the oil in the pressure cooker, add the onion and garlic and fry gently until transparent. Add the spices and cook for 2 to 3 minutes. Stir in the lentils and water. Season with salt and pepper to taste.

Seal the cooker and heat to high pressure. Cook for 7 minutes. Reduce the pressure at room temperature.

Add the yogurt and chutney and stir well. Transfer to a warmed serving dish. Serve hot, with cold meats or curries.

Serves 4

Creamed Swede

750 g (1½ lb)
swede, diced
4 tablespoons water
salt and pepper
50 g (2 oz) butter
3 tablespoons single
cream
2 teaspoons brown
sugar
2 tablespoons
chopped parsley
parsley sprigs to
garnish

Put the swede and water in the
pressure cooker. Season with salt and
pepper to taste.

Seal the cooker and heat to high
pressure. Cook for 4 minutes.
Reduce the pressure at room
temperature.

Drain the swede and mash well.
Beat in the remaining ingredients
and check the seasoning. Transfer to
a warmed serving dish and serve hot,
garnished with parsley.

Serves 4

Vegetable Risotto

250 g (8 oz) brown
rice
salt and pepper
1 litre (1¾ pints)
water
1 onion, chopped
1 green pepper,
cored, seeded and
chopped
3 celery sticks, sliced
75 g (3 oz) butter
3 tablespoons grated
Parmesan cheese
2 tablespoons
chopped parsley
50 g (2 oz) salted
peanuts, chopped
chopped parsley to
garnish

Put the rice, a pinch of salt and
750 ml (1¼ pints) of the water in the
pressure cooker.

Seal the cooker and heat to high
pressure. Cook for 9 minutes.
Reduce the pressure at room
temperature.

Drain and rinse the rice and return
to the cooker. Add the vegetables,
remaining water, and salt and pepper
to taste.

Seal the cooker and heat to high
pressure. Cook for 4 minutes.
Reduce the pressure at room
temperature.

Stir in the remaining ingredients
and transfer to a warmed serving
dish. Serve immediately, sprinkled
with parsley.

Serves 4

Creamed Vegetables

1 kg (2 lb) potatoes,
    halved
2 carrots, thickly
    sliced
1 turnip, quartered
1 parsnip, sliced
1 onion, halved
150 ml (¼ pint)
    water
salt and pepper
2 tablespoons dried
    milk powder
75 g (3 oz) butter
TOPPING (optional):
125 g (4 oz)
    Cheddar cheese,
    grated
3 tablespoons fresh
    breadcrumbs
parsley sprigs to
    garnish

Put all the vegetables, the water, and
salt and pepper to taste in the
pressure cooker.

Seal the cooker and heat to high
pressure. Cook for 5 minutes.
Reduce the pressure quickly.

Drain the liquid from the cooker
and mix 3 tablespoons of it with the
milk powder. Mash the vegetables,
add the milk and butter and check
the seasoning.

If the cheese and crumb topping is
required, transfer the vegetables to
an ovenproof serving dish and
sprinkle with the cheese and
breadcrumbs. Place under a
preheated hot grill until golden
brown.

If serving plain, transfer the
vegetables to a serving dish. Garnish
with parsley and serve hot.

Serves 4 to 6

Pease Pudding

300 g (10 oz) dried
  green peas
600 ml (1 pint)
  water
1-2 bacon or ham
  bones
1 onion, chopped
salt and pepper
2 eggs
50 g (2 oz) butter

Place the peas in a bowl, cover with boiling water and leave to stand for 30 minutes; drain.

Place the water, bones, onion, and salt and pepper to taste in the pressure cooker.

Seal the cooker and heat to high pressure. Cook for 9 minutes. Reduce the pressure at room temperature.

Remove the bones and mash the peas. Beat in the eggs and butter and check the seasoning. Transfer to a greased basin and cover with foil.

Rinse and dry the cooker, put the trivet in position and cover with water. Stand the pudding basin on the trivet.

Seal the cooker and heat to high pressure. Cook for 7 minutes. Reduce the pressure at room temperature.

Turn the pudding out onto a warmed dish to serve.

Serves 4 to 6

Sweet and Sour Beetroot

500 g (1 lb) fresh
  beetroot
3 tablespoons orange
  squash
3 tablespoons vinegar
2 tablespoons brown
  sugar
1 teaspoon cornflour,
  blended with
  2 tablespoons
  water

Put the beetroot in the pressure cooker and add water to a depth of 2.5 cm (1 inch).

Seal the cooker and heat to high pressure. Cook for 15 to 20 minutes, depending on size; allow 30 minutes for very large beetroot. Reduce the pressure quickly.

Peel and dice the beetroot. Place the squash, vinegar and sugar in the cleaned cooker and heat until simmering. Stir in the blended cornflour and bring to the boil. Cook, stirring, until thickened.

Add the beetroot and heat through, stirring. Transfer to a warmed serving dish and serve hot.

Serves 4

Vegetable Curry

1 tablespoon oil
2 tablespoons Madras
   curry powder
300 ml (½ pint)
   water
salt and pepper
1 onion, quartered
500 g (1 lb) carrots,
   sliced
500 g (1 lb)
   potatoes, sliced
3-4 celery sticks,
   sliced
3-4 courgettes, sliced
1 small cauliflower,
   broken into florets
125 g (4 oz)
   mushrooms
1 x 63 g (2 oz)
   packet quick-dried
   peas
4 tomatoes, quartered
4 tablespoons natural
   low-fat yogurt

Heat the oil in the pressure cooker, add the curry powder and cook for 2 to 3 minutes. Cool slightly, then stir in the water. Add salt and pepper to taste and the remaining ingredients, except the tomatoes and yogurt.

Seal the cooker and heat to high pressure. Cook for 6 minutes. Reduce the pressure quickly.

Stir in the tomatoes and yogurt and reheat gently; do not boil. Check the seasoning and transfer to a warmed serving dish. Serve with boiled rice.

Serves 4 to 6

Savoury Lentils

250 g (8 oz) dried
  lentils
600 ml (1 pint) stock
1 onion, finely
  chopped
2 celery sticks, thinly
  sliced
2 tomatoes, skinned
  and chopped
2 tablespoons tomato
  ketchup
1 teaspoon French
  mustard
salt and pepper
chopped parsley to
  garnish

Place all the ingredients, with salt
and pepper to taste, in the pressure
cooker and stir well.

Seal the cooker and heat to high
pressure. Cook for 7 minutes.
Reduce the pressure at room
temperature.

Stir the mixture and check the
seasoning. Transfer to a warmed
serving dish and sprinkle with
parsley.

Serve with gammon or chicken.
Serves 4

Bean Salad with Salami

125 g (4 oz) dried
    red kidney beans
125 g (4 oz) chick
    peas
125 g (4 oz) haricot
    beans
salt and pepper
5-8 tablespoons
    French dressing
3 tablespoons
    chopped mixed
    herbs
1 onion, chopped
125 g (4 oz) salami,
    chopped

Place the kidney beans in one bowl; place the chick peas and haricot beans together in another bowl. Cover with boiling water and leave to soak for 30 minutes; drain.

Put the kidney beans in the unperforated basket, cover with water and place in the pressure cooker. Put the chick peas and haricot beans in the cooker and cover with water. Add salt to taste to both.

Seal the cooker and heat to high pressure. Cook for 20 minutes. Reduce the pressure at room temperature.

Drain the beans and mix together in a salad bowl. Pour over the French dressing and toss together while still warm. Leave to cool.

Add the remaining ingredients, check the seasoning and mix well before serving.

Serves 4 to 6

DESSERTS

Stewed Apple with Honey and Apricots

175 g (6 oz) dried
   apricots
750 g (1½ lb)
   cooking apples,
   peeled, cored and
   quartered
150 ml (¼ pint)
   water
1 tablespoon honey
1 tablespoon orange
   marmalade

Place all the ingredients in the pressure cooker and stir well.

Seal the cooker and heat to medium pressure. Cook for 2 minutes. Reduce the pressure at room temperature.

Turn into a serving dish and serve warm, with whipped cream.
Serves 4 to 6

Creamed Rice with Melba Sauce

50 g (2 oz) butter
600 ml (1 pint) milk
75 g (3 oz) pudding
  rice
125 g (4 oz) sugar
1 x 340 g (12 oz)
  pack frozen
  raspberries,
  thawed
1 tablespoon chopped
  hazelnuts, toasted
  (optional)

Melt the butter in the pressure cooker and tilt to coat the base and sides. Add the milk and bring to the boil. Add the rice and half the sugar and bring back to the boil, stirring. Lower the heat.

Seal the cooker and heat slowly to high pressure. Cook for 12 minutes. Reduce the pressure at room temperature.

To make the sauce: Mash the raspberries with the remaining sugar.

To serve hot: Transfer the rice to an ovenproof dish, place under a preheated medium grill to brown and serve the sauce separately.

To serve cold, turn into a serving dish, leave until cold, then spread the sauce over the surface and decorate with the hazelnuts.

Serves 4 to 6

Crème Caramel

175 g (6 oz) sugar
150 ml (¼ pint)
  water
600 ml (1 pint) milk
1 vanilla pod or piece
  of lemon rind
3 large eggs, beaten

Put 125 g (4 oz) of the sugar and the water in a saucepan. Heat gently, stirring, until dissolved. Bring to the boil and boil until golden brown.

Quickly pour into a buttered 750 ml (1¼ pint) heatproof dish or 4 individual heatproof dishes, tilting so that the caramel coats the sides.

Place the milk, remaining sugar and the vanilla pod or lemon rind in a saucepan and heat gently until lukewarm. Remove the vanilla pod or lemon rind and pour the milk onto the eggs, beating lightly. Strain onto the caramel and cover with foil.

Stand the dish or dishes on the trivet in the pressure cooker and pour in 300 ml (½ pint) water.

Seal the cooker and heat to high pressure. If making one large crème, cook for 6 minutes; cook individual ones for 3 minutes. Reduce the pressure at room temperature.

Leave the crème in the cooker to cool. Loosen the edges and turn out onto a plate just before serving.
Serves 4

Coffee and Orange Upside-Down Pudding

1 orange, thinly
    sliced
2 tablespoons orange
    marmalade
125 g (4 oz)
    self-raising flour
1 teaspoon baking
    powder
125 g (4 oz) soft
    margarine
125 g (4 oz) caster
    sugar
2 eggs
2 tablespoons coffee
    essence

Place the orange slices in a lined and greased 20 cm (8 inch) sandwich tin. Spread the marmalade inbetween.

Sift the flour and baking powder into a bowl, add the remaining ingredients and beat with an electric mixer for 1 minute. Spoon into the tin, taking care to avoid moving the orange slices, and smooth the top.

Cover with 2 sheets of greased greaseproof paper or a sheet of foil, making a pleat across the centre. Secure with string. Pour 600 ml (1 pint) water into the pressure cooker. Stand the basin on the trivet.

Seal the cooker; do not fit weights. Steam for 20 minutes. Put pressure weight on and heat to low pressure. Cook for 15 minutes. Reduce the pressure at room temperature.

Lift the pudding out of the cooker and leave to cool for 10 minutes in the tin, then turn out onto a serving dish. Serve warm, with cream.
Serves 6

Old English Apple Pudding

250 g (8 oz)
  self-raising flour
pinch of salt
125 g (4 oz)
  shredded suet
6-7 tablespoons
  water
750 g (1½ lb)
  cooking apples,
  peeled, cored and
  sliced
175 g (6 oz) brown
  sugar
4-5 cloves

Sift the flour and salt into a bowl, stir in the suet and add enough water to make a soft dough. Knead lightly.

Set aside a quarter of the pastry. Roll out the remainder and use to line a buttered 1.2 litre (2 pint) pudding basin. Fill with layers of apple, sprinkling with the sugar and cloves.

Roll out the reserved pastry into a round for the lid, dampen the edge and put in position, sealing well.

Cover with 2 sheets of greased greaseproof paper or a sheet of foil, making a pleat across the centre. Secure with string.

Stand the basin on the trivet in the pressure cooker and pour in 1.75 litres (3 pints) boiling water. Seal the cooker but do not fit the weight. Steam for 20 minutes.

Put the pressure weight on and heat to low pressure. Cook for 30 minutes. Reduce the pressure at room temperature.

Turn the pudding onto a warmed serving dish. Serve with cream.
Serves 4 to 6

Sussex Pudding

250 g (8 oz)
  self-raising flour
25 g (1 oz) caster
  sugar
pinch of salt
125 g (4 oz)
  shredded suet
6-7 tablespoons
  water
100 g (4 oz) butter
100 g (4 oz) brown
  sugar
6 tablespoons fresh
  breadcrumbs
2 lemons, each cut
  into 6 pieces

Sift the flour, caster sugar and salt into a bowl, stir in the suet and add enough water to make a soft dough. Knead lightly.

Set aside a quarter of the pastry for the lid. Roll out the remainder and use to line a buttered 1 litre (1½ pint) pudding basin.

Soften the butter and mix with the brown sugar and breadcrumbs. Add the lemons and spoon into the basin.

Roll out the reserved pastry into a round for the lid. Cover, cook and serve as for Old English Apple Pudding (above).
Serves 4 to 6

Treacle Sponge

3 tablespoons black
 treacle
125 g (4 oz)
 self-raising flour
1 teaspoon baking
 powder
125 g (4 oz) soft
 margarine
125 g (4 oz) caster
 sugar
2 eggs
1 tablespoon water

Spoon the treacle into a buttered
1.2 litre (2 pint) pudding basin.

Sift the flour and baking powder
into a bowl. Add the remaining
ingredients and beat with an electric
mixer for 1 minute. Turn into the
basin and smooth the top.

Cover and cook as for Old English
Apple Pudding (page 58). Turn out
onto a warmed serving dish and
serve with custard.

Serves 4 to 6

Bread and Butter Pudding

4 slices buttered
  bread, cut into
  strips
50 g (2 oz) sultanas
50 g (2 oz) chopped
  mixed peel
450 ml (¾ pint)
  milk
2 eggs, beaten
50 g (2 oz) sugar

Line a buttered 1.2 litre (2 pint) pudding basin or heatproof dish with bread. Sprinkle with some of the sultanas and mixed peel and cover with a layer of bread.

Repeat the layers until the sultanas, peel and bread are all used, finishing with a layer of bread, placed buttered side uppermost.

Place the milk in a saucepan and heat gently until lukewarm. Pour onto the eggs, stirring constantly, then strain the custard over the bread. Sprinkle with the sugar.

Cover with foil and tie securely with string. Place on the trivet in the pressure cooker and pour in about 300 ml (½ pint) water.

Seal the cooker and heat to high pressure. Cook for 8 minutes. Reduce the pressure at room temperature.

Uncover the pudding and place under a hot grill to brown the top before serving, if preferred.

Serves 4

Christmas Pudding

300 g (10 oz)
   currants
250 g (8 oz) raisins
250 g (8 oz)
   sultanas
50 g (2 oz) glacé
   cherries, chopped
50 g (2 oz) chopped
   mixed peel
25 g (1 oz) blanched
   almonds, chopped
175 g (6 oz) fresh
   breadcrumbs
175 g (6 oz) plain
   flour
175 g (6 oz)
   shredded suet
1 teaspoon each
   ground mixed
   spice, nutmeg and
   cinnamon
175 g (6 oz) soft
   brown sugar
125 g (4 oz) carrot,
   grated
1 tablespoon treacle
4 tablespoons cider
grated rind and juice
   of 1 lemon
2 eggs, beaten
2 tablespoons rum or
   brandy (optional)

Place all the dry ingredients in a large bowl and mix together thoroughly. Add the remaining ingredients and mix well. Leave to stand overnight.

Put the mixture into one 1.2 litre (2 pint) pudding basin or two 600 ml (1 pint) basins and smooth the top.

Cover with 2 sheets of greased greaseproof paper or a sheet of foil, making a pleat across the centre. Secure with string.

Stand the basin on the trivet in the pressure cooker, containing 1.75 litres (3 pints) boiling water. Put the lid on the cooker but do not fit the weight. Steam for 20 minutes.

Put the pressure weight on and heat to high pressure. Cook for 2 hours. Reduce the pressure at room temperature.

Remove the pudding from the cooker. Uncover and leave until cold. Cover with greaseproof paper or foil and store until required.

To reheat the pudding stand on the trivet in the cooker, containing 1.75 litres (3 pints) boiling water. Put the weight on, heat to high pressure and reheat for 20 to 30 minutes, depending on size. Turn out onto a warmed dish to serve.

Serves 8 to 10

Christmas Baked Apples

150 ml (¼ pint)
  water
4 cooking apples,
  cored
3 tablespoons cake
  crumbs
2 tablespoons
  mincemeat
4 teaspoons honey

Pour the water into the pressure cooker and put the trivet in place.

Make a cut in the skin around the middle of each apple. Mix together the cake crumbs and mincemeat and spoon into the core cavity of the apples.

Stand the apples on the trivet but do not let them touch the side of the cooker.

Seal the cooker and heat to high pressure. Cook for 5 minutes. Reduce the pressure at room temperature.

Carefully lift the apples onto a warmed serving dish. Put a teaspoonful of honey on top of each and spoon over the cooking liquor. Serve warm, with cream.
Serves 4

Chicken Paprika

1 tablespoon oil
4 chicken quarters
2 onions, sliced
1 clove garlic, crushed
2 teaspoons paprika
1 x 397 g (14 oz)
    can tomatoes
150 ml (¼ pint) dry
    red wine
salt and pepper
1 tablespoon
    cornflour, blended
    with 2 tablespoons
    water
142 ml (5 fl oz)
    fresh sour cream
    (optional)

Heat the oil in the pressure cooker, add the chicken quarters and fry until evenly browned. Add the onions and garlic and continue cooking for 4 to 5 minutes. Sprinkle in the paprika and cook, stirring, for 2 to 3 minutes. Add the tomatoes with their juice, wine, and salt and pepper to taste.

Seal the cooker and heat to high pressure. Cook for 8 minutes. Reduce the pressure at room temperature.

Check the seasoning, stir in the blended cornflour and bring to the boil. Cook, stirring, until thickened.

Add the cream, if using, and reheat gently; do not boil. Transfer to a warmed serving dish and serve with boiled rice.
Serves 4

Elizabethan Chicken

25 g (1 oz) butter
4 chicken quarters
1 tablespoon plain
  flour
2 onions, sliced
1 teaspoon dry
  mustard
salt and pepper
150 ml (¼ pint)
  chicken stock or
  water
150 ml (¼ pint)
  mead or medium
  sherry
142 ml (5 fl oz)
  fresh sour cream
1 tablespoon flaked
  almonds, toasted,
  to garnish

Melt the butter in the pressure cooker. Toss the chicken quarters in the flour, add to the cooker and fry until golden brown all over. Add the onions and cook for 3 to 4 minutes.

Sprinkle in the mustard, and salt and pepper to taste. Pour in the stock or water and mead or sherry.

Seal the cooker and heat to high pressure. Cook for 18 minutes. Reduce the pressure at room temperature.

Check the seasoning, stir in the cream and reheat gently; do not boil.

Transfer to a warmed serving dish and garnish with the almonds. Serve immediately.
Serves 4

Coq au Vin

25 g (1 oz) butter
4 chicken quarters
125 g (4 oz) bacon,
    derinded and
    chopped
2 onions, sliced
1 clove garlic, crushed
125 g (4 oz) button
    mushrooms
150 ml (¼ pint)
    chicken stock or
    water
300 ml (½ pint) red
    wine
bouquet garni
salt and pepper
1 tablespoon cornflour
TO GARNISH:
4-8 triangles of fried
    bread
1 tablespoon chopped
    parsley

Melt the butter in the pressure cooker, add the chicken quarters and fry until golden brown all over. Add the bacon, onions and garlic and fry for 4 to 5 minutes.

Add the mushrooms, all but 2 tablespoons of the stock or water, the wine, bouquet garni, and salt and pepper to taste.

Seal the cooker and heat to high pressure. Cook for 8 minutes. Reduce the pressure at room temperature.

Blend the cornflour with the remaining stock or water, stir into the sauce and bring to the boil. Cook, stirring, until thickened.

Check the seasoning and transfer to a warmed serving dish. Garnish with the fried bread and parsley. Serve immediately.
Serves 4

Moroccan Chicken

3 tablespoons lemon
juice
1 tablespoon honey
1 teaspoon turmeric
4-6 cloves
pinch of ground
cinnamon
600 ml (1 pint)
water
4 chicken quarters
250 g (8 oz)
long-grain rice
salt and pepper
125 g (4 oz) salted
peanuts
1 orange, sliced, to
garnish

Place the lemon juice, honey,
turmeric, cloves, cinnamon and half
the water in a shallow dish and stir
well. Add the chicken quarters and
leave to marinate for 1 to 2 hours.

Transfer the chicken and marinade
to the pressure cooker. Seal the
cooker and heat to high pressure.
Cook for 8 minutes. Reduce the
pressure quickly.

Remove the chicken and keep
warm. Add the rice, salt and pepper
to taste, and the remaining water to
the cooker.

Seal the cooker and heat to high
pressure. Cook for 8 minutes.
Reduce the pressure at room
temperature.

Stir in the peanuts, then transfer to
a warmed serving dish. Arrange the
chicken on top and garnish with the
orange slices. Serve immediately.
Serves 4

Topside Pot Roast

1 tablespoon olive oil
1.25 kg (2½ lb)
  piece of boned beef
  topside
300 ml (½ pint) beef
  stock
2 tablespoons tomato
  purée
1 teaspoon mixed
  dried herbs
150 ml (¼ pint) dry
  red wine
salt and pepper
2 onions, sliced
4 carrots, sliced
2 leeks, thickly sliced
125 g (4 oz) button
  mushrooms
10-12 black olives
2 tablespoons
  cornflour

Heat the oil in the pressure cooker, add the beef and brown well on all sides. Add all but 4 tablespoons of the stock, the tomato purée, herbs, wine, and salt and pepper to taste.

Seal the cooker and heat to high pressure. Cook for 25 minutes. Reduce the pressure quickly.

Add the vegetables and olives. Seal the cooker and heat to high pressure. Cook for 5 minutes. Reduce the pressure at room temperature.

Lift out the meat and place on a serving dish. Keep warm.

Blend the cornflour with the remaining stock, stir into the cooking liquor and bring to the boil. Cook, stirring, until thickened. Spoon the sauce over the meat and surround with the vegetables. Serve immediately.

Serves 6

Spiced Braised Beef

1 tablespoon oil
750 g (1½ lb) boned beef topside, cut into 4 or 8 slices
2 onions, sliced
300 ml (½ pint) water
2 tablespoons wine vinegar
1 teaspoon ground mixed spice
1 teaspoon French mustard
1 tablespoon tomato purée
salt and pepper
1 tablespoon cornflour

Heat the oil in the pressure cooker, add the beef and fry, turning, until browned on both sides; remove from the cooker and keep warm. Add the onions and fry for 3 to 4 minutes until just beginning to brown.

Add all but 2 tablespoons of the water, the vinegar, mixed spice, mustard, tomato purée, and salt and pepper to taste. Stir well and add the beef.

Seal the cooker and heat to high pressure. Cook for 15 minutes. Reduce the pressure quickly.

Blend the cornflour with the remaining water, stir into the sauce and bring to the boil. Cook, stirring, until thickened.

Check the seasoning and transfer to a warmed serving dish.
Serves 4

Flemish Beef

750 g (1½ lb)
    stewing steak
1 tablespoon plain
    flour
1 tablespoon oil
500 g (1 lb) onions,
    sliced
1 clove garlic, crushed
300 ml (½ pint) beer
2 tablespoons tomato
    purée
1 teaspoon sugar
1 teaspoon mixed
    dried herbs
salt and pepper
TO GARNISH:
8 slices French bread
French mustard
chopped parsley

Cut the meat into 2.5 cm (1 inch) squares. Coat with the flour.

Heat the oil in the pressure cooker, add the meat and fry until evenly browned. Add the onions and garlic and cook until transparent. Stir in the remaining ingredients, adding salt and pepper to taste.

Seal the cooker and heat to high pressure. Cook for 15 minutes. Reduce the pressure at room temperature.

Check the seasoning and transfer the beef to a warmed serving dish. Toast the bread on one side and spread the other side with mustard. Arrange around the beef and serve at once, sprinkled with chopped parsley.

Serves 4

Chilli con Carne

250 g (8 oz) dried
red kidney beans
25 g (1 oz) dripping
1 large onion,
chopped
1 green pepper,
cored, seeded and
chopped
750 g (1½ lb)
minced beef
1 x 397 g (14 oz)
can tomatoes
150 ml (¼ pint)
water
3 teaspoons chilli
powder
1 teaspoon paprika
2 teaspoons sugar
1 tablespoon tomato
purée
2 celery sticks,
chopped

Place the kidney beans in a bowl,
cover with boiling water and leave
for 30 minutes; drain.

Melt the dripping in the pressure
cooker, add the onion and pepper
and fry until just beginning to
brown. Add the beef and fry until
evenly browned, stirring
occasionally.

Add the tomatoes with their juice,
the remaining ingredients and the
kidney beans. Stir well.

Seal the cooker and heat to high
pressure. Cook for 30 minutes.
Reduce the pressure at room
temperature.

Stir well and transfer to a warmed
serving dish. Serve with boiled rice.
Serves 4

Mediterranean Lamb

1 tablespoon olive oil
4 large or 8 small
  lamb chops
1 large onion, sliced
1 clove garlic, crushed
1 aubergine, sliced
1 red pepper, cored,
  seeded and sliced
2 courgettes, sliced
250 g (8 oz)
  tomatoes, skinned
  and quartered
1 teaspoon dried
  rosemary
150 ml (¼ pint) red
  wine
salt and pepper
1 tablespoon
  cornflour, blended
  with 2 tablespoons
  water

Heat the oil in the pressure cooker, add the chops and fry until browned on both sides; remove and keep warm.

Add the onion and garlic to the cooker and fry until transparent. Add the aubergine, pepper and courgettes and cook for 4 to 5 minutes.

Return the chops to the cooker and add the tomatoes, rosemary, wine, and salt and pepper to taste.

Seal the cooker and heat to high pressure. Cook for 15 minutes. Reduce the pressure quickly.

Spoon off any excess fat from the sauce. Stir in the cornflour and bring to the boil. Cook, stirring, until thickened.

Check the seasoning and transfer to a warmed serving dish. Serve with boiled rice or buttered noodles.
Serves 4

Greek Lamb

250 g (8 oz) dried
  butter beans
1 tablespoon olive oil
½ shoulder of lamb,
  weighing about
  1 kg (2 lb)
500 g (1 lb) onions,
  sliced
1 clove garlic, crushed
1 x 397 g (14 oz)
  can tomatoes
1 tablespoon tomato
  purée
1 teaspoon dried
  mixed herbs
10-12 black olives
chopped parsley to
  garnish

Place the butter beans in a bowl, cover with boiling water and leave to soak for 30 minutes; drain.

Heat the oil in the pressure cooker, add the lamb and brown on all sides; remove and set aside.

Add the onions and garlic to the cooker and fry until just beginning to brown. Add the tomatoes with their juice, tomato purée, herbs and butter beans and stir well. Return the meat to the cooker.

Seal the cooker and heat to high pressure. Cook for 20 minutes. Reduce the pressure at room temperature.

Take out the meat, slice and arrange on a warmed serving dish. Stir the olives into the sauce and spoon over the meat. Garnish with parsley and serve with boiled rice.
Serves 4

Lamb and Apricot Sauté

25 g (1 oz) butter
4 large lamb chump
    chops
350 g (12 oz)
    onions, sliced
1 cooking apple,
    peeled and cored
1 x 411 g (14½ oz)
    can apricot halves
    in light syrup
150 ml (¼ pint) cider
    or white wine
    (approximately)
salt and pepper
2 tablespoons
    cornflour, blended
    with 4 tablespoons
    water
114 ml (4 fl oz)
    double cream
    (optional)
chopped parsley to
    garnish

Melt the butter in the pressure
cooker, add the chops and fry until
browned on both sides; remove and
set aside. Add the onions to the
cooker and fry for 4 to 5 minutes.

Return the chops to the cooker
and add the apple. Drain the juice
from the apricots and make up to
300 ml (½ pint) with cider or wine.
Add to the cooker and season to taste
with salt and pepper.

Seal the cooker and heat to high
pressure. Cook for 12 minutes.
Reduce the pressure quickly.

Stir the blended cornflour into the
sauce and bring to the boil. Cook,
stirring, until thickened. Check the
seasoning and add the apricots. Add
the cream, if using, and reheat
gently; do not boil.

Transfer to a warmed serving dish
and garnish with parsley.
Serves 4

73

Fricassée of Veal

25 g (1 oz) butter
750 g (1½ lb) pie
 veal, cubed
300 ml (½ pint)
 chicken stock
bouquet garni
salt and pepper
8-12 button onions
125 g (4 oz) button
 mushrooms
2 tablespoons
 cornflour, blended
 with 4 tablespoons
 water
2 tablespoons lemon
 juice
114 ml (4 fl oz)
 double cream
TO GARNISH:
4 rashers streaky
 bacon, derinded
 and cut in half
parsley sprigs

Melt the butter in the pressure cooker, add the veal and fry gently for 4 to 5 minutes, stirring occasionally. Add the stock, bouquet garni, and salt and pepper to taste.

Seal the cooker and heat to high pressure. Cook for 10 minutes. Reduce the pressure quickly.

Add the onions and mushrooms. Seal the cooker and heat to high pressure. Cook for 5 minutes. Reduce the pressure at room temperature.

Stir in the blended cornflour and bring to the boil. Cook, stirring, until thickened. Check the seasoning and remove the bouquet garni. Stir in the lemon juice and cream and reheat gently; do not boil.

Roll up the bacon pieces and fix with wooden cocktail sticks. Place under a hot grill for 5 minutes until crisp. Remove the cocktail sticks.

Transfer the veal to a warmed serving dish and garnish with the bacon rolls and parsley.
Serves 4

74

Tongue with Hazelnut Sauce

1 ox tongue,
  weighing about
  1.75 kg (4 lb)
1 onion
2 celery sticks
3 bay leaves
2 parsley sprigs
SAUCE:
3 tablespoons
  mayonnaise
3 tablespoons double
  cream, whipped
2 tablespoons
  chopped
  hazelnuts, toasted
salt and pepper
TO GARNISH:
watercress sprigs
lettuce leaves
red pepper slices

Place the tongue in the pressure cooker and cover with cold water. Bring to the boil, remove the tongue and discard the water.

Place the tongue in the cooker and add the vegetables and herbs. Half fill the cooker with water.

Seal the cooker and heat to high pressure. Cook for 15 minutes per 500 g (1 lb). Reduce the pressure at room temperature.

Remove the tongue from the cooker, place in a bowl of cold water and remove the skin, gristle and bones. Dry the tongue on kitchen paper, then form into a round and press into a 15 to 18 cm (6 to 7 inch) round cake tin to fit tightly. Cover with a plate, put a weight on top and leave in the refrigerator for 24 hours.

Combine all the sauce ingredients, adding salt and pepper to taste.

Turn out the tongue, slice and arrange on a serving dish. Garnish with watercress, lettuce and pepper slices. Serve with the sauce.
Serves 6 to 8

Pork and Apple Casserole

25 g (1 oz) butter
4 spare rib pork
   chops
500 g (1 lb) onions,
   sliced
1 clove garlic, crushed
500 g (1 lb) cooking
   apples, peeled,
   cored and sliced
2 tablespoons tomato
   purée
1 tablespoon brown
   sugar
1 tablespoon
   rosemary
salt and pepper
150 ml (¼ pint)
   cider
1 tablespoon
   cornflour

Melt the butter in the pressure cooker, add the chops and fry until browned on both sides. Add the onions and garlic; fry for 2 minutes.

Add the apples, tomato purée, sugar, rosemary, salt and pepper to taste, and all but 2 tablespoons cider.

Seal the cooker and heat to high pressure. Cook for 15 minutes. Reduce the pressure at room temperature.

Transfer the chops to a serving dish and keep hot. Stir the sauce well to break up the apple.

Blend the remaining cider and cornflour together, stir into the sauce and bring to the boil. Cook, stirring, until thickened. Pour over the chops and serve immediately.
Serves 4

Gammon with Peach Sauce

1 kg (2 lb) piece of
   hock or shoulder of
   gammon
2 x 411 g (14½ oz)
   cans peach halves
300 ml (½ pint)
   cider
   (approximately)
3-4 cloves
pinch each of ground
   ginger and
   cinnamon
1 tablespoon
   cornflour, blended
   with 2 tablespoons
   water

Put the gammon in the pressure cooker, cover with cold water and bring to the boil. Remove the gammon and discard the water.

Drain the juice from the peaches and make up to 450 ml (¾ pint) with the cider. Pour into the cooker and add the spices and gammon. Seal the cooker and heat to high pressure. Cook for 25 minutes. Reduce the pressure at room temperature.

Transfer the meat to a serving dish. Strain the liquor and return to the cooker. Stir in the cornflour and bring to the boil. Cook, stirring, until thickened.

Mash half the peaches to a pulp or purée in an electric blender. Stir into the cooking liquor to make a sauce.

Slice the gammon and serve hot or cold, garnished with the remaining peaches. Serve the sauce separately.
Serves 6

Bacon Stroganoff

1 kg (2 lb) piece of
  unsmoked middle
  gammon
25 g (1 oz) butter
1 onion, sliced
1 clove garlic, crushed
250 g (8 oz)
  mushrooms, sliced
½ teaspoon caraway
  seeds
150 ml (¼ pint)
  water
salt and pepper
142 ml (5 fl oz)
  fresh sour cream
chopped parsley to
  garnish

Place the gammon in the pressure
cooker, cover with cold water and
bring to the boil. Drain the gammon
and cut into thin strips. Rinse and
dry the cooker.

Melt the butter in the cooker, add
the onion, garlic and gammon and
fry gently for 5 to 10 minutes. Add
the mushrooms, caraway seeds,
water, and salt and pepper to taste.

Seal the cooker and heat to high
pressure. Cook for 12 minutes.
Reduce the pressure at room
temperature.

Stir in the cream and reheat gently;
do not boil. Transfer to a warmed
serving dish and garnish with parsley.
Serves 6

Pears in Cider

4 pears, peeled
1 tablespoon lemon
   juice
1 tablespoon honey
1 tablespoon
   redcurrant jelly
300 ml (½ pint)
   cider

Stand the pears in the pressure cooker. Mix the remaining ingredients together and pour over the pears.

Seal the cooker and heat to high pressure. Cook for 6 minutes; if the pears are large or very firm allow another 3 to 4 minutes. Reduce the pressure at room temperature.

Arrange the pears in a deep glass serving dish. Pour over the sauce an leave to cool. Chill before serving, with pouring cream if liked.
Serves 4

Honey and Lemon Sponge

3 tablespoons clear
  honey
125 g (4 oz)
  self-raising flour
1 teaspoon baking
  powder
125 g (4 oz) soft
  margarine
125 g (4 oz) caster
  sugar
2 eggs
grated rind and juice
  of 1 lemon

Spoon the honey into a buttered
1.2 litre (2 pint) pudding basin.

Sift the flour and baking powder
into a bowl, add the remaining
ingredients and beat with an electric
mixer for 1 minute.

Turn the mixture into the basin
and smooth the top. Cover with 2
sheets of greased greaseproof paper
or a sheet of foil, making a pleat
across the centre. Secure with string.

Cook as for Old English Apple
Pudding (page 58). Turn the pudding
out onto a warmed serving dish and
serve with cream.

Serves 4 to 6

Chocolate Fudge Pudding

50 g (2 oz) plain
  chocolate
1 tablespoon milk
1 teaspoon instant
  coffee powder
125 g (4 oz)
  self-raising flour
pinch of salt
1 tablespoon cocoa
  powder
125 g (4 oz) butter
125 g (4 oz) caster
  sugar
2 eggs
2 teaspoons grated
  orange rind

Melt the chocolate with the milk and coffee powder in a small basin over pan of hot water.

Sift together the flour, salt and cocoa powder. Cream the butter and sugar until light and fluffy. Beat in the eggs one at a time. Beat in the orange rind, then fold in the flour. Fold in the chocolate mixture.

Turn the mixture into a greased 750 ml (1¼ pint) pudding basin and smooth the top. Cover with 2 sheets of greased greaseproof paper or a sheet of foil, making a pleat across the centre. Secure with string. Stand the basin on the trivet in the pressure cooker and pour in 750 ml (1½ pint) boiling water.

Put the lid on but do not fit the weight. Steam for 25 minutes. Put the weight on and heat to high pressure. Cook for 25 minutes. Reduce the pressure at room temperature.

Turn the pudding onto a warmed serving dish and serve with custard.
Serves 4 to 6

Apricot Fool

125 g (4 oz) dried
  apricots
300 ml (½ pint)
  boiling water
50 g (2 oz) sugar
150 g (5 oz) natural
  low-fat yogurt
175 ml (6 fl oz)
  double cream,
  whipped
1 tablespoon chopped
  hazelnuts, toasted

Put the apricots in a bowl, cover with the boiling water and leave for 10 minutes. Transfer the apricots and liquid to the pressure cooker.

Seal the cooker and heat to high pressure. Cook for 5 minutes. Reduce the pressure quickly.

Add the sugar to the apricots and mix with a fork to dissolve the sugar and break up the fruit. Transfer to a dish and cool, then chill thoroughly

Fold the yogurt and cream into the apricot mixture. Pour into individual glass dishes and chill. Decorate with hazelnuts before serving.
Serves 4 to 6

QUICK PRESERVES

Lemon Curd

4 eggs
grated rind and juice
*   of 3 lemons*
500 g (1 lb) sugar
125 g (4 oz) butter,
*   softened*

Beat the eggs and lemon juice together and strain into a heatproof bowl. Stir in the grated lemon rind, sugar and butter.

Cover the bowl with 2 sheets of greased greaseproof paper or a sheet of foil and place on the trivet in the pressure cooker. Pour in 300 ml (½ pint) water.

Seal the cooker and heat to high pressure. Cook for 10 minutes. Reduce the pressure at room temperature.

Stir the lemon curd and pour into warmed jars. Cover with waxed discs while hot. When cold, cover with cellophane discs or lids.

Store in a cool dry place and use within 6 weeks.
Makes 1 kg (2 lb)

Plum Cheese

500 g (1 lb) plums
5 tablespoons water
500 g (1 lb) sugar

Slit the plums with a knife and place in the pressure cooker with the water.

Seal the cooker and heat to medium pressure. Cook for 5 minutes. Reduce the pressure at room temperature.

Sieve the plums, or remove the stones and work in an electric blender until smooth. Return to the cooker. Stir in the sugar and heat gently until dissolved, stirring constantly. Increase the heat and bring to the boil. Boil rapidly in the open cooker until setting point is reached (see page 84).

Pour into warmed jars and cover with waxed discs while hot. When cold, cover with cellophane discs or lids.

Store in a cool dry place.

Makes approximately 750 g (1½ lb)

Apricot Jam

500 g (1 lb) dried
  apricots
1.2 litres (2 pints)
  boiling water
3 tablespoons lemon
  juice
1.5 kg (3 lb) sugar
50 g (2 oz) **halved
  almonds (optional)**

Place the apricots in a bowl and add the water and lemon juice. Leave to soak for 15 minutes. Transfer the apricots and soaking liquid to the pressure cooker.

Seal the cooker and heat to high pressure. Cook for 10 minutes. Reduce the pressure at room temperature.

Add the sugar and heat gently until dissolved. Increase the heat and bring to the boil. Boil rapidly in the open cooker until setting point is reached (see below). Skim any froth from the jam.

Add the almonds, if using. Leave to cool in the cooker for 15 minutes so that the fruit does not rise. Stir the jam and pour into warmed jars. Cover with wax discs while hot. When cold, seal with cellophane disc or lids. Store in a cool dry place.

Makes approximately 2 kg (4½ lb)
TO TEST FOR SETTING POINT: Spoon a little jam onto a cold plate and draw a finger through the centre. If the mixture stays separate the jam has reached setting point.

Gooseberry and Orange Jam

750 g (1½ lb)
  gooseberries,
  topped and tailed
150 ml (¼ pint)
  water
grated rind and juice
  of 2 oranges
750 g (1½ lb) sugar

Place the gooseberries, water and orange juice in the pressure cooker.

Seal the cooker and heat to medium pressure. Cook for 3 minutes. Reduce the pressure at room temperature.

Add the sugar and heat gently until dissolved. Increase the heat and bring to the boil. Boil rapidly in the open cooker until setting point is reached (see above). Add the orange rind and return to the boil.

Cool, pot and store as for Apricot Jam (above).

Makes approximately 1.25 kg (2½

Apple and Redcurrant Jelly

1.25 kg (2½ lb)
  cooking apples,
  quartered
250 g (8 oz)
  redcurrants
juice of 1 lemon
300 ml (½ pint)
  water
sugar (see method)

Place all the ingredients except the sugar in the pressure cooker.

Seal the cooker and heat to medium pressure. Cook for 4 minutes. Reduce the pressure at room temperature.

Stir the mixture well, then strain through a jelly bag or 3 thicknesses of muslin resting on a nylon sieve. This will take 2 to 3 hours.

Measure the liquid back into the pressure cooker and add 500 g (1 lb) sugar for every 600 ml (1 pint) of liquid. Heat gently in the open cooker, stirring until dissolved.

Increase the heat and bring to the boil. Boil rapidly until setting point is reached: Take the cooker off the heat and place a spoonful of the mixture on a cold plate; if a skin forms the jelly will set.

Pour the jelly into warmed jars and cover with waxed discs while hot. When cold, seal with cellophane discs or lids. Store in a cool dry place.
Makes approximately 1.5 kg (3 lb)

Mint Jelly

75 g (3 oz) mint
1 kg (2 lb) cooking
  apples, quartered
600 ml (1 pint)
  water
2 tablespoons lemon
  juice
sugar (see method)
green food colouring
  (optional)

Pick all the young leaves from the mint (approximately half the mint), chop and reserve. Place the stalks and other leaves in the pressure cooker. Add the apples, water and lemon juice

Seal the cooker and heat to medium pressure. Cook for 4 minutes. Reduce the pressure at room temperature.

Stir the mixture well, then strain and continue as for Apple and Redcurrant Jelly (above). When setting point is reached, add the reserved mint and colouring and bring back to the boil. Finish as for Apple and Redcurrant Jelly.
Makes approximately 1.5 kg (3 lb)

Bitter Orange Marmalade

750 g (1½ lb)
  Seville oranges
1 lemon
600 ml (1 pint)
  water
1.5 kg (3 lb) sugar

Squeeze the juice from the oranges and lemon and place in the pressure cooker. Reserve the pith and pips and place on a piece of muslin. Tie up to form a bag and add to the cooker. Slice the orange and lemon rinds thinly and add to the cooker. Pour in the water.

Seal the cooker and heat to high pressure. Cook for 15 minutes. Reduce the pressure at room temperature.

Remove the muslin bag and leave to cool. Squeeze all the juice into the cooker. Add the sugar and heat gently, stirring until dissolved.

Increase the heat and bring to the boil. Boil rapidly until setting point is reached: Take the cooker off the heat and place a spoonful of marmalade on a cold plate; if the mixture stays separate when a finger is drawn through the centre, the marmalade will set.

Skim if necessary. Leave for 15 minutes so that the peel does not rise, then pour into warmed jars. Cover with waxed discs while hot. When cold, seal with cellophane discs or lids. Store in a cool dry place.
Makes approximately 1.75 kg (4 lb)

Grapefruit and Lemon Marmalade

500 g (1 lb)
  grapefruit
500 g (1 lb) lemons
500 ml (1 pint)
  water
1.5 kg (3 lb) sugar

Thinly pare the grapefruit and lemon rinds. Slice finely and place in the pressure cooker. Squeeze the juice from the fruit and add to the cooker. Reserve the pith and pips and place on a piece of muslin. Tie up to form a bag and add to the cooker. Pour in the water.

Seal the cooker and heat to high pressure. Continue as for Bitter Orange Marmalade (opposite).
Makes approximately 1.75 kg (4 lb)

Green Tomato Chutney

450 ml (¾ pint)
  malt vinegar
350 g (12 oz)
  onions, finely
  chopped
1 kg (2 lb) green
  tomatoes,
  quartered
500 g (1 lb) cooking
  apples, peeled and
  cored
250 g (8 oz)
  sultanas (optional)
1 teaspoon salt
1 teaspoon ground
  ginger
1 teaspoon pickling
  spice, tied in
  muslin
350 g (12 oz) brown
  or white sugar

Place half the vinegar, the onions, tomatoes, apples, sultanas, if using, salt and spices in the pressure cooker

Seal the cooker and heat to high pressure. Cook for 10 minutes. Reduce the pressure quickly.

Add the remaining vinegar and the sugar and heat gently, stirring, until dissolved. Increase the heat and bring to the boil in the open cooker. Simmer, uncovered, over a low heat for 15 minutes or until the chutney thickens.

Remove the muslin bag and pour the chutney into warmed jars. Cover with waxed discs while hot. When cold, cover with cellophane discs or lids. Store in a cool dark place.
Makes approximately 1.5 kg (3 lb
NOTE: When bottling chutney, do not allow metal tops to come into contact with the chutney as the vinegar may cause them to corrode.

Marrow Chutney

1 kg (2 lb) marrow,
  peeled, seeded and
  diced
salt
600 ml (1 pint) malt
  vinegar
500 g (1 lb) cooking
  apples, peeled and
  cored
250 g (8 oz) onions,
  chopped
1 teaspoon pickling
  spice, tied in
  muslin
¼ teaspoon ground
  ginger
250 g (8 oz) raisins
250 g (8 oz)
  demerara sugar

Place alternate layers of marrow and salt in a large bowl and leave for several hours. Drain well.

Put half the vinegar, the marrow, apples, onions, spices and raisins in the pressure cooker and stir well.

Seal the cooker and heat to high pressure. Cook for 10 minutes. Reduce the pressure quickly.

Stir in the remaining vinegar and the sugar and continue as for Green Tomato Chutney (above).
Makes approximately 1.5 kg (3 lb)

Rhubarb and Ginger Chutney

00 ml (1 pint) malt
 vinegar
kg (2 lb) rhubarb,
 thickly sliced
50 g (8 oz) onions,
 chopped
50 g (8 oz) cooking
 apple, peeled and
 cored
teaspoon salt
teaspoon pickling
 spice, tied in
 muslin
teaspoon ground
 ginger
50 g (12 oz) brown
 sugar
0 g (2 oz)
 crystallized
 ginger, chopped
 (optional)

Place half the vinegar, the rhubarb,
onions, apple, salt and spices in the
pressure cooker.

Seal the cooker and heat to high
pressure. Cook for 10 minutes.
Reduce the pressure quickly.

Add the remaining vinegar and the
sugar and continue as for Green
Tomato Chutney (opposite).

When the chutney has thickened,
stir in the crystallized ginger, if
using, and bring back to the boil.

Pot as for Green Tomato Chutney.
Makes approximately 1.5 kg (3 lb)

Spiced Prune Chutney

500 g (1 lb) prunes
500 g (1 lb) cooking
    apples, peeled,
    cored and sliced
1 large onion,
    chopped
300 ml (½ pint)
    malt vinegar
1 teaspoon curry
    powder
1 teaspoon ground
    mixed spice
1 teaspoon salt
350 g (12 oz) brown
    sugar

Place the prunes in a bowl, cover with boiling water and leave for 30 minutes. Drain and place in the pressure cooker. Add the remaining ingredients, except the sugar.

Seal the cooker and heat to high pressure. Cook for 10 minutes. Reduce the pressure at room temperature.

Stir in the sugar and heat gently until dissolved, stirring constantly. Continue as for Green Tomato Chutney (page 90).

Makes approximately 1 kg (2 lb)

Tomato Sauce

1.25 kg (2½ lb)
    tomatoes,
    quartered
350 g (12 oz) onion,
    chopped
450 ml (¾ pint)
    malt vinegar
125 g (4 oz) sugar
1 teaspoon ground
    ginger
2 teaspoons salt
1 teaspoon dry
    mustard
6 cloves

Place all the ingredients in the pressure cooker and stir well.

Seal the cooker and heat to high pressure. Cook for 15 minutes. Reduce the pressure quickly.

Sieve the mixture and return to the cooker. Bring to the boil, lower the heat and simmer, uncovered, until the sauce has reduced to the required thickness, stirring occasionally.

Pour into a bowl to cool. When cold pour into screw-top jars, but do not fill right to the top: the sauce must not touch the metal lids.

Makes approximately 900 ml (1½ pints)

Pickled Pears

00 ml (1 pint)
 white wine or
 distilled malt
 vinegar
 teaspoon pickling
 spice, tied in
 muslin
-4 cloves
 tablespoon lemon
 juice
 kg (2 lb) sugar
 kg (4½ lb)
 under-ripe pears,
 peeled, cored and
 quartered

Place all the ingredients, except the pears, in the pressure cooker. Heat gently, stirring constantly, until the sugar has dissolved. Add the pears.

Seal the cooker and heat to high pressure. Cook for 25 minutes. Reduce the pressure at room temperature.

Remove the pears with a slotted spoon and place in preserving jars.

Bring the cooking liquid to the boil and boil, uncovered, for 10 to 15 minutes until well reduced. Strain and pour over the pears, covering them completely.

Seal the jars and leave for a month before using.

Makes approximately 2 kg (4½ lb)

INDEX